W9-BYA-220

Hang Out Under the Shady Canopies with

CHIMPANZEES

Published by Wildlife Education, Ltd.
12233 Thatcher Court, Poway, California 92064
contact us at: **1-800-477-5034**
e-mail us at: **animals@zoobooks.com**
visit us at: **www.zoobooks.com**

Printed in China

ISBN 1-888153-52-0

Chimpanzees

Series Created by
John Bonnett Wexo

Written by
Ann Elwood

Scientific Consultant
Jane Goodall, Ph.D.
The Jane Goodall Institute for Wildlife Research, Education and Conservation

Art Credits

Paintings: Richard Orr

Additional Art:

Page Twenty: Lower Left, Map, Charles Byron

Pages Twenty and Twenty-one: Top, Walter Stuart; **Portrait of Jane Goodall:** Darrel Millsap

Back Cover: Richard Orr

Photographic Credits

Front Cover: Royalty Free *(Getty Images)*

Pages Six and Seven: Wolfgang Bayer *(Bruce Coleman, Inc.)*

Page Nine: Helmut Albrecht *(Bruce Coleman, Inc.)*

Page Ten: Hugo Van Lawick *(Caracal Limited)*; **Upper Right,** Geza Teleki, Ph.D.

Page Eleven: Top, Middle, and Bottom, Toni Angermayer, DG.Ph. *(Photo Researchers)*

Pages Twelve and Thirteen: Royalty Free *(Getty Images)*

Page Fourteen: Hugo Van Lawick *(Caracal Limited)*

Page Fifteen: Left, Hugo Van Lawick *(Caracal Limited)*; **Right,** Royalty Free *(Getty Images)*

Page Sixteen: Lower Left, Tom McHugh *(Photo Researchers)*; **Middle,** Royalty Free *(Getty Images)*

Page Seventeen: Top, K&K Ammann *(Bruce Coleman, Inc.)*; **Bottom,** Royalty Free *(Getty Images)*

Pages Eighteen and Nineteen: Royalty Free *(Getty Images)*

Page Twenty: Lower Left and Middle, Hugo Van Lawick *(Caracal Limited)*; **Right,** Geza Teleki, Ph.D.

Page Twenty-one: Worldwide Photos, Inc.

Pages Twenty-two and Twenty-three: Royalty Free *(Getty Images)*

Back Cover: Royalty Free *(Getty Images)*

On the Cover: A Chimpanzee

Contents

Chimpanzees and humans are alike in many ways. A baby chimp laughs when its mother tickles it. After chimpanzees fight, they kiss and make up. When one chimpanzee comforts another, it gives it a hug or a pat on the back. Chimpanzee anatomy differs very little from human anatomy, and chimpanzees are considered the most intelligent of the apes. Like humans, they have the ability to plan ahead.

Along with humans, chimpanzees belong to the order of animals called primates. Others in this group include gorillas, orangutans, gibbons, monkeys, lemurs, and bush babies. But only chimpanzees share so many of our abilities and behavioral traits. Dr. Jane Goodall has studied chimpanzees for several decades. Early in her studies she discovered that chimps make tools and solve problems. It was once thought that these were abilities that only humans had.

There are, of course, many ways that chimpanzees and humans are different. Chimpanzees are smaller and stronger than humans. An adult male chimpanzee stands three or four feet tall and weighs about 100 pounds. But a chimpanzee can lift more weight than a man who is six feet tall.

All wild chimpanzees live in Africa—mostly in thick rain forests and in woodlands. There are two types, or species, of chimpanzee—the common chimpanzee and the bonobo, also known as the pygmy chimpanzee. There are far fewer bonobos than there are common chimps. Bonobos are considered the most intelligent of the two species and are thought to have more in common with humans.

You might think that because chimps are so much like us we would let them live in peace. But we don't. Because of human activities, chimpanzees may one day exist only in zoos. Wild chimpanzees are rapidly disappearing. To save the chimpanzees that remain, something must be done soon!

COMMON CHIMPANZEES

A chimpanzee's body is made for climbing and swinging in the trees. With its long arms, a chimp can easily reach from branch to branch. And with its flexible hands and feet, it can grab and hook on to them. Because of this ability to reach and hang on, a chimpanzee can travel across thin branches without breaking them.

In many ways, chimpanzees' bodies are a lot like ours. Like us, chimps do not have tails. They have no hair on their faces or on the palms of their hands or the soles of their feet. They have fingernails and toenails, instead of claws or hooves. And, perhaps most important of all, chimps have big brains.

Like a kid on a jungle gym, a chimp can move through the trees by swinging from branch to branch. This way of moving is called *brachiation*.

A chimp's feet are really like an extra pair of hands. Using their thumb-like big toes, chimps can wrap their feet around a tree trunk or a branch. So when climbing, they can grip with *both* their feet and their hands.

It's easy to tell the two types of chimps apart. Bonobos are slightly smaller than common chimps. And they usually have a part running down the middle of their heads. Sometimes their hair even sticks out sideways!

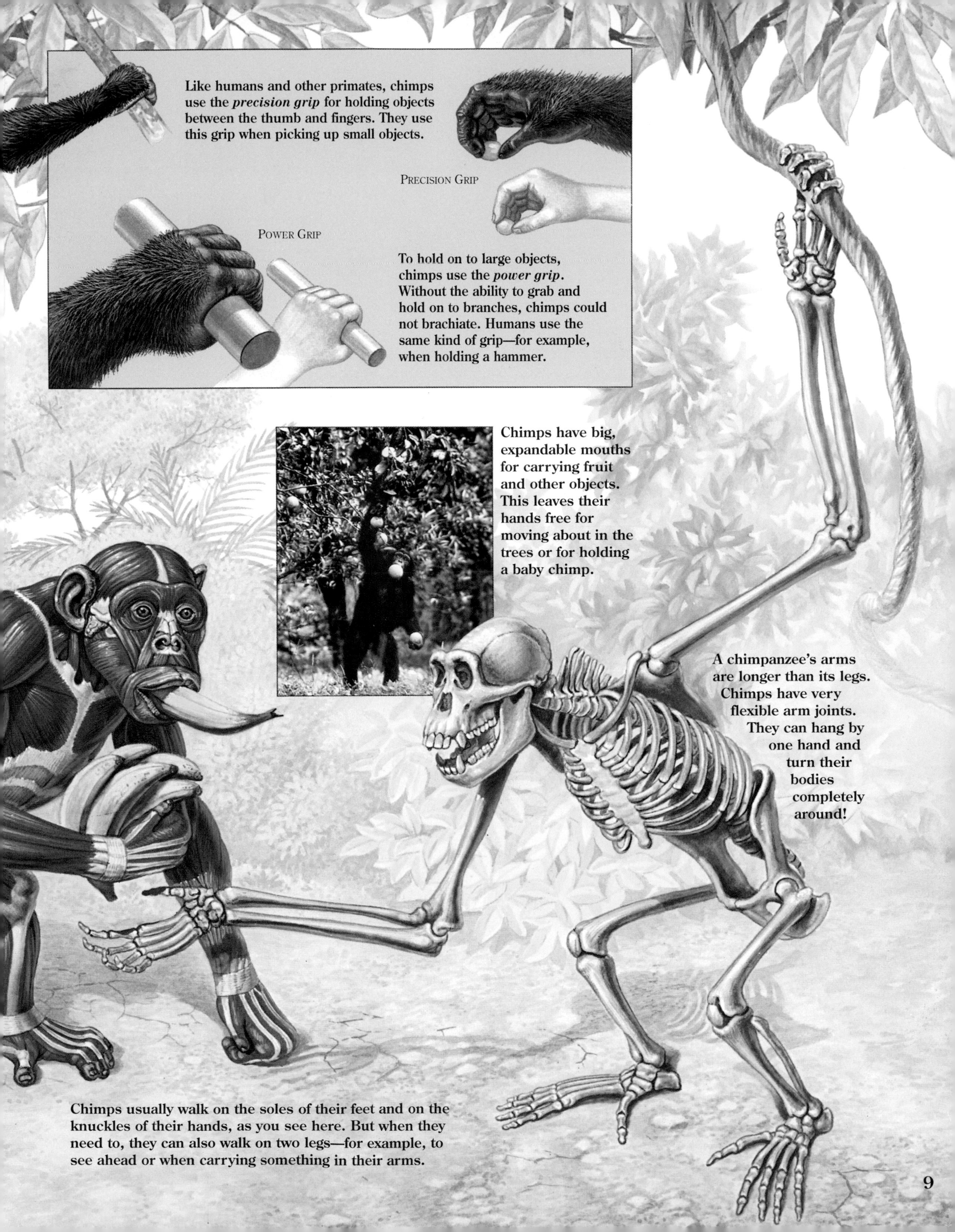
Like humans and other primates, chimps use the *precision grip* for holding objects between the thumb and fingers. They use this grip when picking up small objects.
PRECISION GRIP
POWER GRIP
To hold on to large objects, chimps use the *power grip*. Without the ability to grab and hold on to branches, chimps could not brachiate. Humans use the same kind of grip—for example, when holding a hammer.
Chimps have big, expandable mouths for carrying fruit and other objects. This leaves their hands free for moving about in the trees or for holding a baby chimp.
A chimpanzee's arms are longer than its legs. Chimps have very flexible arm joints. They can hang by one hand and turn their bodies completely around!
Chimps usually walk on the soles of their feet and on the knuckles of their hands, as you see here. But when they need to, they can also walk on two legs—for example, to see ahead or when carrying something in their arms.

Chimps belong to large groups, or *communities*. But they also spend much of their time in small groups, looking for food and socializing. Chimps can be very loving, and they can be very aggressive when necessary.

Each chimp holds a rank—or place—in the community. Usually, one male holds the top rank. He leads fights against predators, or against chimpanzees from other territories. Sometimes the group tries to scare strangers away by calling loudly and charging fiercely. Chimps have even been known to attack and kill strangers. But within their own community, chimps are much gentler with each other, although they do sometimes quarrel. After a quarrel, often within half an hour, they make up by holding a hand out to the other and kissing. The tension in the community is relieved, and the others offer consolation with pats and hugs.

Chimps have many ways of communicating with each other in their complex society.

Chimpanzees are noisy animals. They have more than *30 different calls* to communicate with each other. The chimps above are "hooting"—probably to let their friends know where they are. A chimp's hoot can be heard up to *two miles away*!

Chimpanzees often share their food with each other. When a chimp finds a tree with lots of fruit, he may call the others to a feast. While eating, chimps grunt to show how happy they are.

While the males are displaying, the females and babies stay out of the way. Male chimps become so excited that they could hurt somebody without meaning to.
Male chimpanzees shake branches, throw rocks, and charge each other in a display meant to intimidate others and demonstrate superiority. The male that puts on the fiercest display becomes (or remains) the leader. Eventually, another chimp—or a group of chimps—will challenge and overthrow him.
Chimps show their feelings with gestures, noises, and facial expressions. There may be genuine smiles or happy faces, nervous grins, or grins that say, "Let's be friends again," and pouts to express disappointment. Chimps have many signals to tell each other how they feel, to warn each other of danger, and to report where food is.
Chimps eat mostly fruit, leaves, seeds, and flowers. But they will also feast on ants, honey, eggs, caterpillars, birds, and sometimes small animals, even—rarely—other chimps.
Celery
Meat
Fruit
Nuts
Leaves
Eggs
Roots
Bananas
Seeds
Insects

Chimps love babies. The whole community is excited when a baby is born. Older chimps tolerate a lot of mischief and teasing from infants. They even let the babies jump on them!

Chimps usually have only one baby every five or six years. A female chimp could give birth to as many as five infants in her lifetime, but it's more likely that she will raise a maximum of three.

A baby chimp weighs three to four pounds at birth. It will drink its mother's milk and share her nest until it is weaned at four or five years old. Like human children, chimps take a long time to grow up. This is because they have a great deal to learn. They need to learn how to get around on their own, how to find food that is safe to eat, how to fight and display, how to make nests, and how to avoid danger. They learn many of these skills by playing.

For the first three months of its life, a chimp baby is quite helpless. But it *can* grip tightly to its mother as she moves from place to place. If a baby loses its grip or slips, it just whimpers softly and its mother quickly holds it close.

Young chimps like to be tickled, and they laugh when someone tickles them. In this picture, a mother chimp tickles her baby.

A common chimpanzee is born with a pale, pinkish-yellow face. Its skin turns darker after a few years. The shape of its face also changes—it grows longer, and the mouth and chin get bigger.

A bonobo is born with a black-skinned face. Its skin stays black all of its life. But, like the common chimp, the shape of its face changes, too.

All chimps hate rain. Yet, for some reason, they usually stay out in the open during a downpour. This baby has jumped into its mother's arms to keep from getting too wet.

When chimps are about eight or nine years old, they begin to leave "home" for a few days at a time. But they remain close to their mothers throughout their lives.

Young chimps love to wrestle and chase each other through the trees. By playing together, youngsters learn how to act in chimp society.

Young chimps are curious and intelligent. Like human toddlers, they explore everything—from mud to butterflies. Older chimpanzees watch them carefully to make sure they don't get into trouble.

At night, chimps build nests in trees to keep themselves safe from leopards and other predators. Mothers and babies sleep together.

To build a nest, a chimp makes a platform "mattress" of broken leafy branches. Then it bends twigs over the platform to make it soft and springy. All of this takes only about five minutes.

C himpanzees use many different objects as tools. They use twigs to fish for termites, leaves to soak up water, and rocks to throw at enemies. A few other animals also use objects as tools. Sea otters, for example, use rocks to crack open clams.

But chimpanzees are the *only* animals—except humans—that can make tools. They can take an object and change it into something useful. Once scientists thought that toolmaking was something that only *people* could do. But, as you will see below, chimps can also solve problems by using tools. They could not do this without their intelligence and their flexible hands.

To fish for tasty termites, which live inside big mounds, a chimp makes a tool out of a twig. First he selects the twig carefully. Then he strips the leaves from the stem.

1

2

The chimp uses the twig to probe inside the termite mound. The termites then lock their jaws around the twig.

When a chimp wants a drink, it will sometimes make a sponge from a leaf. It crumples the leaf by chewing it, and then dips it into the water. A chimp can get seven or eight times more water this way than by dipping its fingers into a pool.

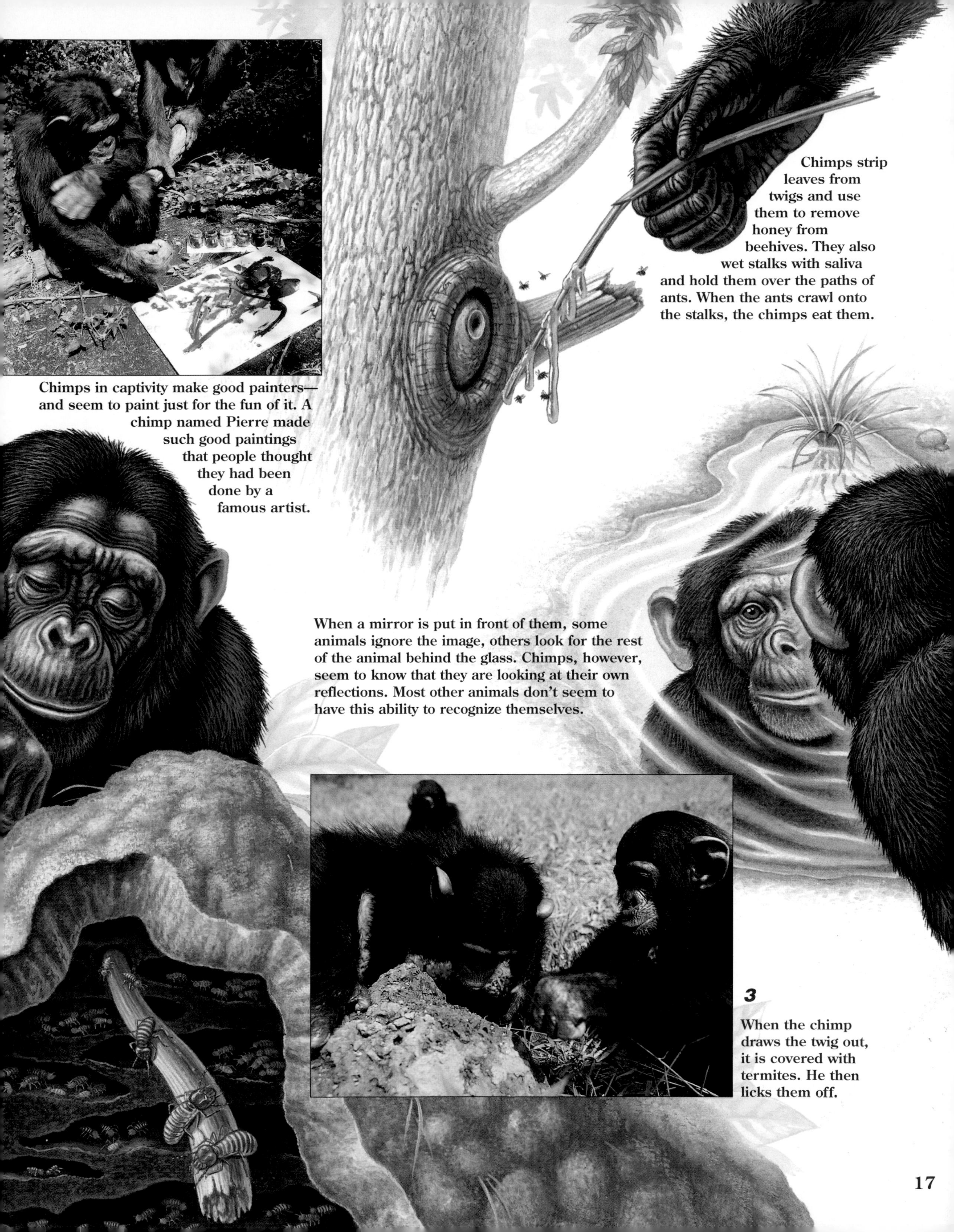

Chimps in captivity make good painters—and seem to paint just for the fun of it. A chimp named Pierre made such good paintings that people thought they had been done by a famous artist.

Chimps strip leaves from twigs and use them to remove honey from beehives. They also wet stalks with saliva and hold them over the paths of ants. When the ants crawl onto the stalks, the chimps eat them.

When a mirror is put in front of them, some animals ignore the image, others look for the rest of the animal behind the glass. Chimps, however, seem to know that they are looking at their own reflections. Most other animals don't seem to have this ability to recognize themselves.

3

When the chimp draws the twig out, it is covered with termites. He then licks them off.

Common chimpanzees

When Jane Goodall was a child, it was her dream to study animals in Africa and write about them. And that is what she does. Before she began observing chimpanzees in the wild in 1960, very little was known about their habits. She has made many exciting discoveries about chimpanzees since that time. She still spends several months each year in the forest at Gombe National Park in Tanzania, Africa, where she and her assistants study the wild chimpanzees that live there.

Dr. Goodall worries about the future of chimpanzees. She makes speeches all over the world to raise money for chimps and to teach people to respect and learn from them. She and several other scientists want to change the way chimpanzees are treated.

To find out what you can do to help, write to: The Jane Goodall Institute for Research, Education and Conservation, 8700 Georgia Avenue, Suite 500, Silver Spring, MD 20910, or go to www.janegoodall.org.

To catch one wild infant chimp, many other chimps are killed. Once captured, the chimps are put into small wooden crates to be shipped out of Africa. Many die on the journey. For every chimp that reaches its destination, up to 10 others may die.

Dr. Goodall observes chimpanzees. Then she writes down or tapes what she sees and hears. Because she is trained, she sees things that other people might not see. What do you think is happening in the chimp group at the right?

AFRICA

KNOWN AREAS

PROBABLE AREAS

POSSIBLE AREAS

Chimpanzee numbers are declining, and the chimp is extinct in parts of its former range. The map above shows where chimps live today.

FLO

MCGREGOR

WORZLE

Jane Goodall learns to tell one chimp from another. She gives each one a name and records his or her life. Above are three of the chimps she has studied.

Chimps seem to like being on stage—so they make good entertainers. But is it right to turn an animal into a trained clown just to please humans? Are chimps meant to ride bicycles, or are they meant to live free in the wild?

Jane Goodall was the first scientist to discover that chimpanzees hunt other animals for food. When one chimp has meat, the others hold out their hands to beg for a share. They usually get it.

In 1961, a chimp astronaut named Ham was fired in a spaceship 155 miles into the sky. When he landed, people shook his hand and called him a hero. After that, he spent the rest of his life in zoos, mostly alone.

Jane Goodall also discovered that chimps make and use tools. The chimp below has made a twig into a fly whisk by chewing the ends to spread out the fibers.

Sometimes chimps quarrel with each other, usually over food. But when they do, they have ways of making up, like hugging and kissing.

Jane Goodall has found that loving care, especially from their mothers, is very important to young chimpanzees. Female chimps that don't get good care as infants never learn how to be mothers themselves.

The chimpanzees' future depends on humans learning to live in harmony with them. Chimpanzees share many "human" traits. In some cases, these traits put chimpanzees in jeopardy. Because they are so similar to humans, many chimpanzees are captured for research and study to aid human medicine.

Another danger for chimpanzees is that people in Africa sometimes hunt them for food or to protect crops. When parts of the forest are cleared for farming, chimpanzees suddenly live closer to humans. When caught stealing food from the farmers' gardens, the chimps can be hurt or killed.

The biggest threat to chimpanzees is the destruction of their forest homes. Commercial logging destroys the forest or leaves patches too small to provide security and food for the chimpanzees in the region. Chimpanzees live in the areas where they were born. When their habitats are destroyed or broken into small pieces, the chimps become too isolated. And moving to a new area is dangerous.

If you move away from your neighborhood and friends and go to a new school, you may be sad for a while, but you will soon make new friends. Chimpanzees can't adjust to the loss of their home. If they move into the territory of other chimpanzees, they will be attacked by resident chimps protecting their homes and families. Many chimpanzees will die. So you see, it's very important that chimpanzee habitat be preserved.

Some chimpanzees are protected on reserves in parts of their range, but are still hunted by poachers. The bonobo, or pygmy chimpanzee, is the only great ape that does not have any national park or reserve. Although it is protected by law in the only place it occurs—the Democratic Republic of the Congo (formerly Zaire)—the law is not enforced. Infant bonobos are sometimes taken as pets or given as gifts to foreign dignitaries. This, too, depletes the chimpanzee population.

Without major efforts to change the situations that harm them, all chimpanzees could be extinct in 100 years or less. Surveys to identify different chimpanzee groups, chart where they live, and count the population size are important first steps to help chimpanzees. Reserves must be established for protection. Where reserves exist, they must be guarded against poachers. Where protective laws are in place, they must be enforced.

Finally, conservation education programs are needed in Africa to reduce the hunting of our fellow primates. You help just by learning about chimpanzees and conservation. The more people who learn and care, the better the chimpanzee's chances for survival.

Index